CHRISTIAN SOUL

FOUNDATIONAL PRINCIPLES OF FAITH

CLIFFORD YOUNG, JR.

outskirts
press

Christian Soul
Foundation Principles of Faith
All Rights Reserved.
Copyright © 2021 Clifford Young, Jr.
v2.0

The opinions expressed in this manuscript are solely the opinions of the author and do not represent the opinions or thoughts of the publisher. The author has represented and warranted full ownership and/or legal right to publish all the materials in this book.

This book may not be reproduced, transmitted, or stored in whole or in part by any means, including graphic, electronic, or mechanical without the express written consent of the publisher except in the case of brief quotations embodied in critical articles and reviews.

Outskirts Press, Inc.
http://www.outskirtspress.com

ISBN: 978-1-9772-4036-1

Cover Photo © 2021 Jeannie Shumate Halverson, Shumate Design Associates
All rights reserved - used with permission.

Outskirts Press and the "OP" logo are trademarks belonging to Outskirts Press, Inc.

PRINTED IN THE UNITED STATES OF AMERICA

Table of Contents

Acknowledgments and Dedication	v
Foreword	vii
Introduction	ix
1. Christianity 101	1
Beyond the Basics	6
2. Connection to Christ	10
The Call to Connection	13
Growing Your Faith	14
3. Your Soul	18
Make the Most of Your Uniqueness	22
4. Connecting with Mankind	23
Forgiveness	32
5. The Walk	35
6. The Dance	39
My Dance	40
Do the Dance	41
7. The Armor	43

8. A New Hope	51
Eternal Life	55
9. You Have Idols	58
10. Finding A Church	62
The Word	63
Worship	63
Prayer	64
Fellowship	65
11. Sharing Your Soul	67
Bible Versions	71

Acknowledgments and Dedication

Thank you to those who were instrumental in helping me write this manuscript. Thank you to Carolyn Jerry for editing and making my words and thoughts clear, concise and captivating. Thank you to my great friends and mentors: Pastor George Baum, Chris Van Duyn, MariaBella Soriano, Rev. Dr. Samuel Fillon, Dr. Keith Matthews, the late Dr. Henry T. Sampson and the late Glen Johnson. I have learned from you the importance of living a life dedicated to the Lord Jesus in surrender and authenticity with my neighbor.

Thank you church family at New Hope Christian Center for giving me the opportunity to make mistakes in ministry and recover. I look forward every day to shepherding you all with the grace and love of Jesus Christ. Thank you Dad, Dr. Clifford O'Dell Young, Sr. for your continued support and friendship through all of my life's transitions. Thank you Mom, Dr. Laura Howzell Young-Sampson, for your encouragement, verbal and financial. The sacrifices that you have made for me and my family are great and I hope to do the same and more for you. Thank you, Robin, my wife, for all that you do in my life and for all that you are to me. Without you this book, my first, would not be possible. You shape me because you see me at my worst and my best and you still love me. I am blessed to share this life with you and I look forward to many more years of marital bliss. Oneness!

This book is dedicated to my children, Clifford O'Dell Young, III and Catheryn Olivia Young. I love you and you both are my pride and joy. Thank you for putting up with me as I continue to figure out what it means to have a Christian Soul and pass it down to you. May the Lord continue to bless you as you venture through this life with Him as your focus and guide.

Foreword

Soul...Soul food? Soulmate? Soul train? Maybe...

Soul seems to involve creation, imagination, connection, animation.

You know it when you see it.

Soul is the very *essence* of a person when reflecting his/her Source, connecting with others. Soul makes words jump off the page and dance. Soul animates folks near and far, sets toes tapping, hearts jumping and minds spinning (Genesis 1).

Soul seems to require the right connection in order to discover its gifts. Cliff Young has that connection: In music, yes —he sets a choir on fire, piano keys dance when Cliff comes out to play. When he proclaims the Word, soul echoes in every other soul in the house. And there is a soul in his home — just get yourself invited over for 'black spaghetti.'

Cliff sings loud and proud with praise –connecting us to our Source. And now here he comes bringing a book and his soul with him: animating holy words, bringing them to life, awakening our own souls.

So sit back and let your soul have a read, connect, and reflect your Source. See the images come forth. Let your life be animated by these good words from my 'son,' brother, and friend.

Now get ready for some soul because Clifford Young Jr. is in the house!

George Baum
Senior Pastor
Captain's Wheel
Rolling Hills Estates, CA

Introduction

I HAVE SEEN in my lifetime a variety of "Christians." Some who recognize Jesus on Easter and Christmas and rarely consider Christ at any other time of year. I have seen families that attend church regularly, have all the answers to the questions, but their lives are a mess. And I have had the pleasure of knowing Christians who seem to be at peace no matter what storms come along. In this book you will see what it is to be a Christian and how to have the peace of God that surpasses all understanding.

The term soul has a vast meaning and has been interpreted in a variety of ways. Together we will explore this term from a Christian point of view, primarily using the Bible, Old and New Testament, as a resource. The Bible remains the most popular book ever written and is full of wisdom that remains applicable from ancient times until now.

<u>To the New Christian</u>: Welcome to the family! You may not be experiencing changes in your life yet but I can promise you that God is there and working. I pray that this book will be a tool that moves you forward in your faith and walk with God.

<u>To the seeker:</u> I am thrilled that you are looking for answers in your life. There are so many worldly points of view that can confuse you. I pray this book brings clarity to your search and that you come to know the one true God deeply, intimately and without hesitation. God loves you and wants to be part of your life.

<u>To the long-time Christian:</u> The concepts in this book will probably not be new to you. However you may benefit particularly from Chapter 11: Sharing Your Soul. I pray that you will pass this book along to a new believer or a seeker to help them with their walk. Thank you for working with me toward fulfilling the Great Commission.

Chapter 1

CHRISTIANITY 101

"Then he said to the crowd, "If any of you wants to be my follower, you must give up your own way, take up your cross daily, and follow me."

-Luke 9:23

THERE ARE A few basic beliefs that define Christianity. The primary belief is that Jesus Christ is the one and only Son of God. Christians believe that Jesus Christ, who was without sin, took the place of all sinners when He died on the cross. Most importantly Christians believe that Jesus rose from the grave three days after his death, that He was seen by many witnesses, that He was taken up to heaven and now sits at the right hand of His Father, God.

Christians also believe in the trinity, referred to as the Godhead. Father, Son, and Holy Spirit are one and the same and yet hold different functions. The Father is seen as the architect of life and creation. The Son is seen as the representation in the flesh of the Godhead that physically sacrificed himself to bring us to the Father. The Holy Spirit is the consciousness of God and helps us communicate daily with the Godhead. These functions are interchangeable and not exclusive to each member. The trinity is a mystery because we, with finite minds, cannot fully comprehend the relationship –but let's try. Let's use water, H^2O, to help us grasp the concept of the Trinity. Water can have three forms: solid, liquid or gas. God the Father is the unwavering foundation part of the trinity. He is represented by the solid, the ice. God the Son, Jesus, is represented by liquid, able to move or soak into any crevice. God the Holy Spirit is represented by gas, mist or steam and able to give the moisture that envelopes you. Each one is unique and yet they are all the same, H^2O.

Prayer, fellowship, worship, study, giving, communion and baptism are all major foundational principles of the Christian faith. We call these tenets or rites of the Church. I will briefly discuss each rite.

Prayer is basically communication to, with and from God. It is very important in the life of a believer. The Bible teaches Christians to "Pray without ceasing" (1 Thessalonians 5:17), meaning that we are to pray in all situations. We are not called to just make a list of problems for God to solve. Prayer also includes acknowledgment of God, adoration of God, petition to God and affirmation of God's power. The sample prayer given to the disciples by Jesus includes all of these elements and therefore serves as the Christian's basic prayer.

> *Our Father which art in heaven*
> *Hallowed be thy name.*
> *Thy kingdom come.*
> *Thy will be done, as in heaven, so in earth.*
> *Give us day by day our daily bread.*
> *And forgive us our sins;*
> *for we also forgive every one that is indebted to us.*
> *And lead us not into temptation;*
> *but deliver us from evil. (Luke 11:2-4, KJV)*

Prayer can be done with or without others. It is the basic means of building one's faith in and relationship with God.

Worship is also a form of prayer to God. It can be done with or without other people. Worship takes on many forms and it is considered to be a way of life rather than an act. Christians believe that their life is worship to God. In the Old Testament the most prominent form of worship was animal sacrifice. One would kill an animal and offer up a burnt offering to God as an act of worship. In the days of the New Testament, after Jesus Christ became the ultimate sacrifice for the world, Christians' began worshiping in other ways. Singing, dancing, writing, drawing, playing instruments, helping and serving others are all ways to worship God.

Fellowship or the gathering of believers is a foundational principle of the Church. Ever since the death and resurrection of Jesus Christ, the Church Body has gathered together to practice these principles and rites of the church together. Prayer and worship can be done individually but fellowship is done in community. Fellowship is not just a suggestion, it is a must. Hebrews 10:25 (KJV) says not to forsake *"the assembling of ourselves together, as the manner of some is; but exhorting one another: and so much the more, as ye see the day approaching."*

Fellowship is important for believers because it activates the fruit of the Spirit found in Galatians 5:22-23. Without fellowship, one does not have the opportunity to learn how to love another in a safe environment.

Study of Scripture is also a principle that is often done in the company of believers. One of the most popular ways of study and application by Christians is corporate Bible study. It is true that one can study alone but there is always something (the Bible, literature, audio tape, video) to study that adds another "voice," therefore making the study a community experience. Other forms of Bible study are sermons or homilies by ministers or pastors. These are usually incorporated into a church service, though many churches have adopted a weeknight for in-depth study, leaving Sunday morning services for topical study. Sunday school for youth and adults before service has also been an option for churches.

Giving is encouraged in all fellowships and is a command from God. Church ministry would not exist if believers did not give. The Apostle Paul in 2 Corinthians 9:6-8 says, *"Remember this — a farmer who plants only a few seeds will get a small crop. But the one who plants generously will get a generous crop. You must each decide in your heart how much to give. And don't give reluctantly or in response to pressure. 'For God loves a person who gives cheerfully.' And God will generously provide all you need. Then you will always have everything you need and plenty left over to share with others."* When one is not able to give monetarily, giving of time or talent is always an option. Christians believe that all of our resources come from and belong to God. Therefore, Christians give back to God and act as managers or stewards of God's money.

Communion, also called the Lord's Table, is the act of remembering Jesus Christ and His sacrifice for the World. Jesus instituted this rite. Luke 22:17-20 (NIV) says, *"After taking the cup, he (Jesus) gave thanks and said, 'Take this and divide it among you. For I tell you I will not drink again from the fruit of the vine until the kingdom of God comes.' And he took bread, gave thanks and broke it, and gave it to them, saying, 'This is my body given for you; do this in remembrance of me.' In the same way, after the supper he took the cup, saying, 'This cup is the new covenant in my blood, which is poured out for you.'"* Communion is an outward expression of belief in Jesus Christ done in community. The elements of bread and wine represent the body and blood of Jesus Christ.

Baptism is another expression of an outward sign of commitment to Jesus Christ. Jesus Christ was baptized by John the Baptist before he started His ministry. Matthew 3:13-15 says, *"Then Jesus went from Galilee to the Jordan River to be baptized by John. But John tried to talk him out of it. 'I am the one who needs to be baptized by you,' he said, 'so why are you coming to me?' But Jesus said, 'It should be done, for we must carry out all that God requires.' So John agreed to baptize him."* Although all Christians believe that baptism is important, we occasionally disagree on how and when it should be done. Some believe that babies should be baptized while others believe that baptism should take place after the age of accountability. Some churches believe in full submersion into a pool or body of water, while others believe that "sprinkling" or pouring of water on the head is sufficient. Although the traditions are different, all believe that baptism is an outward sign of new life in Christ.

Though "what" we do and "why" we do it has not changed over the centuries, I find that their meaning is not explained in the 21st century as often as it has been in centuries before. Christians have done an inadequate job of passing down meaning about these rites to future generations. This becomes a problem when faith is challenged or someone questions Christian faith. What does a Christian believe or do when his or her faith in God is challenged?

Beyond the Basics

Hebrews 11:6 says, *"And it is impossible to please God without faith. Anyone who wants to come to Him must believe that God exists and that He rewards those who sincerely seek Him."* We acknowledge God by knowing that He is paying attention to us (all-knowing), is always present (everywhere), has our best interests in mind (all-loving) and can work on our behalf (all-powerful). This does not mean that God is a "deified" Santa Claus or personal genie. Christians believe that God works according to His will, not ours. The sooner we understand this, the better. Jesus demonstrated this in the Garden of Gethsemane on the way to the cross. In talking with God the Father Jesus says, *"My Father! If it is possible, let this cup of suffering be taken away from me. Yet I want your will to be done, not mine"* (Matthew 26:39). In that passage, Jesus shows us how we are to acknowledge God the Father.

A Christian is one who adores God. *"God is Spirit, and those who worship Him must worship in spirit and truth"* John 4:24 (NKJV). I love to adore my wife, Robin. Adoring her builds her self-esteem and confidence and benefits me by reinforcing in my mind, heart and soul how much she means to me. When we adore God, our soul connects with the Spirit of God and the truth of His Word. This gives us a connection that exceeds even the deepest of relationships: connections between wife and husband or connections between parent and child. His Spirit connects with our spirit, enabling us to worship God with all of our heart, soul and strength (Deuteronomy 6:5). The Spirit is also the revealer of wisdom and understanding in the Word of God. The Spirit opens the *truth* of God's Word to us. Therefore, we adore God through the Spirit of God in the *truth* of God's Word. We recorded a classic song for our Christian Soul CD called "Open The Eyes Of My Heart" written by Michael W. Smith. As we usually do, we added our own "Al Green" Living Sacrifice twist to the song. This is one that I think can bring you closer in your relationship with God. Talk to Him about your desire to connect and be close to Him. He will most certainly answer that request.

A Christian is one who confesses to God. *"But if we confess our sins to him, he is faithful and just to forgive us our sins and to cleanse us from all wickedness"* (1 John 1:9). Confession is necessary if one desires to be a Christian. Confession is one of the reasons Christ died for us. In the Garden of Eden, God wanted Adam to confess his sin. Adam did not, but blamed Eve and God for his sin. God then turned to Eve for her to confess. She did not, but blamed the serpent and God as well.

Through all of scripture, God seeks a man or woman to confess. God loved King David and I believe one of the reasons God called David a man after his own heart (1 Samuel 13:14) was because of his tendency to confess sin. As an example, Psalm 51 is a Psalm of David focused on confession. After his adultery with Bathsheba and murder of her husband, Uriah, David writes, *"Have mercy on me, O God, according to your steadfast love; according to your abundant mercy blot out my transgressions. Wash me thoroughly from my iniquity, and cleanse me from my sin!" (Psalm 51:1-2 ESV).* We are to keep short accounts with God and regularly confess all sin that is committed. God has a way of gently teaching us and bringing to light ways that we have sinned either recently or in the past. As He brings them to your mind, take them to God's heart.

There are many more details of the Christian faith that could be discussed. Since that exceeds the scope of this book, if you have more questions about the Christian faith that I have not addressed you might enjoy *Mere Christianity* by C.S. Lewis or *The Good And Beautiful God Series* by James Bryan Smith. If you are not a believer, I would like to encourage you to explore the Christian faith more. One way to do this is to ask a Christian to tell you the story about their faith. You might also attend a church service or sit in as a guest at a Bible study. Feel free to ask questions. We may not always have the answers but we can work together to find them.

Chapter 2

Connection to Christ

"Yes, I am the vine; you are the branches. Those who remain in me, and I in them, will produce much fruit. For, apart from me you can do nothing."

John 15:5

We can believe in Christ and choose not to follow Him. Does Christ become the Him or him? That capital "H" makes all the difference in the world. Do you choose to make Christ Jesus Lord of your life or is He just another historical person? John 15:5 begs the question: Is Christ the vine that brings meaning to your life or is He just another branch?

Life is full of choices. From the time we wake up in the

morning until the time that we go to sleep, we make choices. Even after we are asleep, our bodies continue to make choices. According to Google we each make 35,000 conscious decisions a day! Connection with Christ is a choice. Jesus says, *"...Whoever wants to be my disciple must deny themselves and take up their cross and follow me"* (Matthew 16:24, NIV). This is the connection. This is what the soul longs to have. The ultimate desire of our soul is to follow Christ Jesus.

The best way to understand connection may be to talk about the opposite: disconnection. When you want the lamp to turn on and it doesn't, you check the connection. If the lamp is disconnected then it's obvious because the cord is unplugged. When you are disconnected from Christ, what does that look like?

Allow me to share a bit of my story. The late '80s was the day of gangster rap music with influences like NWA (Niggas' With Attitudes), Ice T and Too Short. Rap music influenced the whole culture. Everybody wanted to act like these characters. Gone were the days of clean and good-hearted rap music. The music promoted fornication, drugs, drinking, womanizing, murder, prison, lack of respect for authority and many other vices. I wanted to be part of the culture but I did not want to live the life of a gang member. I wanted the popularity but not the pain. I began to use my musical talent and make "mixed tapes" of the popular music of the time. I even changed my name to "Cliffy Dee." Though the culture was more into hard core or gangster rap music, I tended to lean toward the moderate rap like the music of Will Smith, known at the time as the "Fresh Prince." This was my pace: girls, good-natured fun, loyal friends and being the life of the party. I wanted to live like the rap group "Kid n' Play" from the popular Newline Cinema *House Party* movies. Life was a party to me. This is how I was able to make it and transition from the structure of elementary school at the military academy to Christian middle school. I had no interest in being a "church boy" at the time. I went to church but did not have any kind of relationship with my maker. I just wanted to have fun. "Religious activity" was all church was to me, just an activity I had to do. Through my adolescent years, Christ was knocking. I didn't want to answer the door. Through my college days, Christ was knocking. I still didn't answer the door. I was behaving like a 2 or 3-year old who tells their parents "I can do it myself!" or "Et' me do it!" I was concerned about all I would have to give up if I answered the door. I suppose I didn't trust that God would be able to take care of things better than I was doing myself. When I got married I finally let Christ into every aspect of my life and He changed me.

As an adolescent I could feel the disconnect but I didn't recognize what it was. I wanted to do what I knew to be good but the pull to do wrong, to sin, was very prevalent in my bones. Paul talks about this pull in Romans 7:15 NIV *"I do not understand what I do. For what I want to do I do not do, but what I hate I do."* I felt God pulling me in his direction but I did not want to lose all the fun that I was having in the world. I was resisting the connection. Because I resisted, I kept seeking the next fun thing, the next adrenaline rush, the next relationship. Each of those things brought happiness but the feeling was short lived and not very satisfying. Like seeing a delicious-looking dessert, gobbling it up and almost immediately feeling let down because it wasn't as satisfying as you thought it would be.

When I finally gave in and allowed Jesus Christ to be the Lord of my life, it was like plugging in the lamp. Everything started to work the way it was supposed to. The connection to God brought me authentic Joy. When I worshipped God, it wasn't just a religious exercise. I genuinely felt the peace of God and the joy of God that lasts, instead of the fleeting moments of pleasure the world brings. I began changing my behavior because I simply didn't need the rush anymore. The connection I had with God had replaced the false pleasure I'd been seeking in the world.

THE CALL TO CONNECTION

What does Jesus say about Connection? Let's recall the verse stated at the beginning of the chapter. John 15:5 tells us, *"Yes, I am the vine; you are the branches. Those who remain in me, and I in them, will produce much fruit. For apart from me you can do nothing."* This is one of Jesus' last teachings to his disciples. A few chapters later Jesus is arrested and on His way to the Cross. We need Him in order to live a life that is pleasing to God the Father, beneficial to us and also beneficial to mankind. God the Father wants us to "Be Holy." Ephesians 1:4 tells us that God chose us before the foundation of the world to be holy. Holiness is the nature of God and something we cannot live up to. We need Jesus Christ, the perfect one, to be our Savior, advocate and friend to intervene for us through this life. But it is not all up to Him. We need to choose to connect. Jesus promises that as we connect with Him our burdens will become light. Matthew 11:28-29 says, *"Come unto me, all ye that labor and are heavy laden, and I will give you rest. Take my yoke upon you, and learn of me; for I am meek and lowly in heart: and ye shall find rest unto your souls."*

Today is the day to find your connection with God and develop your relationship with him. If you are not feeling connected with God, the first step is to begin reading the Bible. Read his love letter to you and allow Him to share His heart with you. Let me suggest that you start with the Book of Genesis, the first book of the Bible, or the Gospel of Luke, the third book of the New Testament. These books read like a good story and will capture your heart. Take the time to read the Word of God and be changed.

Growing Your Faith

The book of Hebrews, chapter 11, gives us some great insight about faith. The very first sentence tells us *"Now faith is confidence in what we hope for and assurance about what we do not see."* The book goes on to commend Abel (one of Adam and Eve's sons) and Enoch (who was taken to heaven without passing through death) for being men who pleased God because of their strong faith. We are then told *"And it is impossible to please God without faith. Anyone who wants to come to him must believe that God exists and that he rewards those who sincerely seek him" (Hebrews 11:6).* If you are new to being a Christian the idea of faith may seem unfamiliar to you. Actually, I would argue, it is not as unfamiliar as you might think. As I write this book I have faith that the computer upon which I'm typing this will not give out and erase this document. I have faith that the chair I am sitting in will hold me. I trust that I will be able to breathe in and out and take steps as I always have. I believe by faith that it will happen. Having faith is actually a very natural aspect of human life. Without faith we would be paralyzed and unable to accomplish anything. We have confidence and trust that the world will function the way it always has because we have a lifetime of history –evidence. In the same way that a baby develops a trust in his mother and father that his needs will be met, we develop trust as we grow in our relationship with Christ. You may not feel totally sure that Christ will be able to meet your needs, that He loves you unconditionally or that He wants to spend eternity with you. Here's the great news. Matthew 17:20 reassures us with these words from Jesus: *"I tell you the truth, if you had faith even as small as a mustard seed, you could say to this mountain, 'Move from here to there,' and it would move. Nothing would be impossible."* If you have ever seen a mustard seed you know that it is very tiny. Jesus wants you to know that even a tiny bit of faith is full of great power. As you practice connecting with Christ over the coming months and years, your mustard seed faith will grow and grow, eventually becoming a strong oak tree that cannot be shaken.

The writer of the book of Hebrews in chapter 11 talks about many men and women of faith. Christians call this chapter the "Hall of Faith." If you're ever feeling doubt about your faith this is a great chapter to turn to. As you read the chapter you get various pictures of the men and women who believed God and depended on Him to bring them through. Some of them were kings. Some of them were poor. Some of them were popular. Some of them were marginalized. With God, it doesn't matter who you are or where you come from. Just like all of those people, you are one of God's wonderful creations and you are able to grow your faith in God.

I am drawn to music and enjoy writing music. It helps me to connect with Christ. When I think of growing faith based on history I think of all the stories in the Bible that demonstrate God's faithfulness. I encourage you to find music that reminds you of God's faithfulness and love for you and listen to it regularly to help remind you of the faith that is growing inside you. One of the songs I've written with my amazing co-writer, MariaBella Soriano, is called "Cross Over Now." You can hear the song on our CD *Beauty is to Worship*. Here are some of the lyrics:

Do you remember O child of God, what the good Lord can do
Parted the Red Sea, made it dry land, children of God walked through
Do you remember O child of God, what the good Lord can do
He Healed the leper, sight to the blind, He made the lame dance too

Cross over now, He loves you so,
He'll never leave, He won't let go
He'll lead You through this Jordan too
Cross Over Now, He promised you

Chapter 3

―∽―

Your Soul

"...You must love the Lord your God with all your heart, all your soul, and all your mind."

Matthew 22:37

WHEN I THINK about the soul, many word pictures come to my mind. Being a musician, I automatically think about music and all of the artists who brought soul to their genre. Frank Sinatra, Luciano Pavarotti, Ludvig Van Beethoven, Dolly Parton, James Brown, Aretha Franklin...The list goes on and on. When they sing or play an instrument, their performance appeals to your soul. My favorite ambassador of soul is one of music's finest: composer, educator and trumpet player Wynton Marsalis. He is a soul-bearer of all genres of music, from very early European classical music to the latest style of Jazz music. When Marsalis speaks and performs, you can feel the soul that he is. Whether he speaks or communicates in any form, there is soul.

Christians believe that there is a supreme being that created heaven and earth (Genesis 1). This supreme being also created man and woman in the image of Himself. (Genesis 2) In addition, Christians believe that all creation is subject to this supreme being (John 1) and that, one day, they will live in paradise with this being who created them and longs to have a relationship with them (Revelation 21-22). Christians believe that God loves us so much that he gave His only Son as a sacrifice in order to redeem fallen humanity (John 3:16). It is with this understanding that Christians believe that everyone has a soul. Everyone! If you are a human, you have a soul. Having a soul is a gift from God given to humanity from the very beginning. Genesis 2 says, *"Then the Lord God formed the man from the dust of the ground. He breathed the breath of life into the man's nostrils, and the man became a living person"* (Gen 2:7). God breathed into man's nostrils a soul. Soul is called the breath of life in this passage. Notice also that God breathed in man's nostrils, not his mouth. The nostrils are made to filter out impurities in the air and provide our lungs with adequate amounts of oxygen to inspirit the mind and body. It is no mistake that God breathed into the nostrils.

Although the soul is intangible, everyone knows it when they hear it, see it, feel it or experience it. Soul is, in part, an experience of the senses: your eyes, nose, ears and touch. When God created your soul, He made you unique. Because of your uniqueness you have gifts given to you by God that may look similar to others but are not because you are very different. Being unique is very important for the overall functioning of mankind. If we were all the same there would be parts of our world that would not function properly. We need everyone's unique gifts, everyone's unique soul. We are made in the image of God and we are the only creation with a soul.

Imagine an orchestra with only wind instruments. Sure the oboes, flutes and the clarinets would sound lovely but there would be no depth without the strings, the brass instruments and the percussion. All of the parts are necessary to create the complete, beautiful, unique sound of the orchestra. Take a listen to Beethoven's 5th symphony and you can hear the complete sound of soul in the orchestra. You can think of all of mankind as the orchestra and you are one of the important instruments that help to make beautiful music.

One of the most popular Psalms of the Bible, Psalm 23, a Psalm of David says, *"The Lord is my shepherd; I shall not want. He makes me lie down in green pastures; He leads me beside quiet waters. **He restores my soul**"* (Ps 23:1-3, NASB). When Jesus was despairing as he faced the cross to be crucified for the sin of the world he said, *"**Now is my soul troubled**; and what shall I say? Father save me from this hour: but for this cause came I unto this hour"* (John 12:27 KJV).

God is deeply concerned with your soul.

I wrote a song titled "Even Till the End of All Time" in my mid-twenties. It was a time when I was first starting to experience the concept of why God loves me and how God loves me. The words are simple:

Lover of my Soul, fill me with joy overflowing.
You're the Prince of Peace. Love is yours. Life comes from You.
For me to know Father, Son, Spirit in You.
For me to be part of your wonderful family.
For me to know you love me so.
Even Till the End of All Time.

This song is all about what one needs to know regarding God's love for us. Notice that it does not answer the questions of why and how. The song answers who God is, and what He does. He is the Lover. He fills us. He is the Prince of Peace. Love belongs to Him. Life comes from Him. All He requires is that we know Him, not understand Him. He wants us to be part of His plan and His family for eternity.

Who we are as a soul is generated by the Spirit of God, who communicates to believers in God. A believer in God has the Holy Spirit living inside. When you believe and accept Jesus as Lord of your life, the Holy Spirit is deposited into your life to help guide you into a life of holiness. Non-believers also have a soul but that soul is directed by the will of the person instead of the will of God. The conscience of the non-believer is the only guide that directs.

The Christian soul that is led by the Holy Spirit has the supernatural power of the Godhead to intervene in those things that will cause harm to the soul. The soul of the non-believer has only the physical and mental strength it can muster alone to fight off the pull to sin.

MAKE THE MOST OF YOUR UNIQUENESS

The song "Heart and Soul" is one of the first songs kids learn to play on the piano. It is usually taught by rote and played with at least one other person. Imagine that this song demonstrates the relationship that God desires to have with each and every unique human being. God wants to play the foundational lower notes. He keeps the rhythm, the pace, the flow and he allows us to create the top melody with the unique creativity He has given us. We have to communicate with God in order to make the song harmonious and pleasant. Our song won't sound like anyone else's song. Sometimes we hit a "clinker" and lose our harmony but as long as we go right back to communicating with our creator, the one who plays the foundation, we can get back on track.

In the book of Matthew, chapter 22, one of the Pharisees asked Jesus "which is the greatest commandment in the Law?" Jesus said *"You shall love the Lord your God with all your heart, and with all your soul, and with all your mind."* The soul of God communicating with the individual souls of humans is a harmonious, creative musical masterpiece. Life!

Chapter 4

CONNECTING WITH MANKIND

"A servant of the Lord must not quarrel but must be kind to everyone, be able to teach, and be patient with difficult people."
2 Timothy 2:24

GOD PROVIDES OPPORTUNITIES for us to connect with our neighbor. Who are our neighbors? Those with whom you come into contact on your life journey. Does this mean that you are responsible to every human being on earth? No! Each of us has a sphere of influence, people with whom we develop relationships in the various parts of our lives. Each of those people has another sphere of influence so the effect of our influence is multiplied by the number of people with whom we communicate and connect.

Christians need to be under the influence of the Holy Spirit who produces Spiritual Fruit. Paul says, *"But the Holy Spirit produces this kind of fruit in our lives: love, joy, peace, patience, kindness, goodness, faithfulness, gentleness, and self-control. There is no law against these things!" (Galatians 5:22-23).* God, the Holy Spirit, helps the believer with producing the fruit of the Spirit.

Have you ever bit into a delicious piece of fruit? My favorite fruit is good, juicy, seedless watermelon. I live in California and on a hot summer's day there is nothing like sinking your teeth into a sweet, red, juicy piece of watermelon. If the watermelon vine didn't produce a watermelon, if there was never any fruit, the farmer would pull it out by the roots and get rid of it. If it doesn't fulfill its purpose he doesn't need it. In the same way if it produces scrawny little watermelons, or if they are bitter, then the vine is not fulfilling its purpose. Believers are called to grow the fruit inside of them. Not scrawny or bitter fruit but beautiful, delicious, sweet fruit: love, joy, peace, patience, kindness, goodness, faithfulness, gentleness, and self-control. These characteristics are the evidence of a believer fully under the control of the Holy Spirit. This is what the Christ follower should want to be. We all start with tiny fruit that needs to grow. Just like the farmer who must tend to his crops, providing mineral-rich soil, water and sunlight, we also must nurture our fruits and help them grow. If we neglect them, they will simply dry up and disappear.

With this understanding, let's take a look at each particular fruit and its meaning:

Love: the first and all-encompassing word with which Paul starts the list. This is the highest form of love that is sacrificial in nature. This is love that gives, even one's own life, for the sake of another. *"For God so loved the World that he gave…"* (John 3:16). Christians are to love each other the way that God loved us.

However, real love has conditions. God's love is not unconditional. In the Old Testament God has a set of conditions that He gives to the nation of Israel. *"Hear, O Israel: The Lord our God is one Lord: And thou shalt love the Lord thy God with all thine heart, and with all thy soul, and with all thy might"* (Deuteronomy 6:4 KJV). This command is a condition. The chapters go forward to explain the blessings of following the conditions and the cursing that will come by not following the conditions. The Children of Israel serve as reminders of God's conditions throughout the ages.

In the New Testament the condition does not go away by any means. In John 14:21 Jesus says, *"Those who accept my commandments and obey them are the ones who love me. And because they love me, my Father will love them. And I will love them and reveal myself to each of them."* The most famous verse in the Bible, John 3:16, also has a condition. *"For God so loved the world, that he gave his only begotten Son, that whosoever believeth in him should not perish, but have everlasting life."* The condition for us in this verse is to believe.

The book of Job is about a man of great faith and integrity. God gave Satan permission to test Job's faith by taking away everything he had. His animals were stolen and his farm hands were killed. His sheep and all the shepherds were burned to death. His camels were stolen and his servants killed. His house collapsed on all of his children and killed them. To top it all off, Satan brought a terrible skin disease upon Job. These were terrible things but Job remained faithful. But the next part is what I want to focus on.

When three of Job's friends heard of the tragedy he had suffered they traveled together from their homes to console him. Job's friends grieved with him and threw dust into the air to show their grief. Then they sat with him for seven days and nights. No one said a word to Job. His friends just sat and grieved with him. They were simply there for Job in his time of grief. That is the incredible love of friends. We will stop the story right there because the story of love changes when they start to criticize Job and attempt to call out his sin. But for the first part of the story we can say that these Old Testament friends were observing a New Testament principle from the apostle John. *"Dear friends, let us continue to love one another, for love comes from God. Anyone who loves is a child of God and knows God. But anyone who does not love does not know God, for God is love"* (1 John 4:7-8).

Joy: In the Old Testament, the book of Nehemiah talks about having Joy. The Jewish people had the task of rebuilding the wall that had been destroyed when they were taken into exile. When the people came together after building, they looked at the law books, the first five books of the Bible. The people discovered that they were very far away from the ideal that God had for them and they were very sad. Nehemiah encouraged the Jewish people with these words. *"Go and celebrate with a feast of rich foods and sweet drinks, and share gifts of food with people who have nothing prepared. This is a sacred day before our Lord. Don't be dejected and sad, for the joy of the Lord is your strength!"* (Nehemiah 8:10). The joy that we are talking about brings strength regardless of the situation. Joy is not fake. It endures through happy times and sad times. It is as strong as love. Joy gives the connotation of rejoicing and being glad regardless of the situation you are facing. Paul in Philippians says *"Rejoice in the Lord always: and again I say, Rejoice"* (Philippians 4:4 KJV). Think of this: every situation you've faced you have made it through to the other side. You have made it through all of the frustrations, the sad times, and the challenging times you've faced. You're still here! Your own life experience tells you that nothing lasts forever and that there will be joy on the other side of the crisis. The difference as a Christian is acknowledging, before the crisis has ended, that you know God's got this. Romans 8:37 says, *"Despite all these things, overwhelming victory is ours through Christ, who loved us."* He will walk through the dark valleys with you and there will be joy again.

In the Old Testament, the book of Jeremiah chapter 31, talks about how God will bring the people of Israel back to Him. He promises to rebuild Israel and that *"You (Israel) will again be happy and dance merrily with your tambourines."* God promises that He will *"turn their mourning into joy."* He will do the same for Christians who are trusting God for their future. As you grow in your faith and develop your connection with God you'll find that your trust in His plan for your life will grow too. You can relieve yourself of the burden of controlling every little thing that happens by giving it over to God and having the confidence that whatever the current crisis is will eventually come to an end. This gives us a reason to *"Rejoice in the Lord always."*

Peace: This is the peace that one can only experience with God. Jesus says, *"I am leaving you with a gift — peace of mind and heart. And the peace I give is a gift the world cannot give. So don't be troubled or afraid"* (John 14:27). This does not mean you will never worry about anything again. You're human and one of the downfalls of being human is that we fall into worrying sometimes. As a Christian we can go to God with our worries, lay them at His feet, and be confident that God cares enough that He will take care of it. Sometimes we find ourselves picking up the worry again and so we go back to God in prayer and, once again, lay our worry down. The more we do this the greater the fruit becomes. We can get so good at it that we can help others to also lay their worries down. In Philippians 4:6-7 we read, *"Don't worry about anything; instead, pray about everything. Tell God what you need, and thank him for all he has done. Then you will experience God's peace, which exceeds anything we can understand."* When you are filled with God's peace there will be evidence in your life. You won't need to focus on the troubles this life brings. Thus you will be able to brush off the little things that bothered you in the past. You will have confidence that your future is held in the hands of the Creator of the universe and that brings peace. People will enjoy being around you because you have a positive attitude and a calm spirit. Your connections with other people will become richer, deeper and more satisfying.

Love, Joy and **Peace** are the three foundational pieces of fruit from the Holy Spirit. The next six pieces of fruit emerge out of the three.

Patience: This is the kind of patience that is long-suffering. It represents a state of emotional calm in the face of provocation or misfortune. Proverbs 25:15 tells us *"Patience can persuade a prince, and soft speech can break bones."* This is a difficult fruit to develop. I have been told to never pray for patience because God will give me extra opportunities to practice! Our key verse at the beginning of this chapter tells us to *"be patient with difficult people"* (2 Timothy 2:24). I suppose there is little need to be patient with people who are cooperative; everyone can do that. In our most difficult relationships we are called to be patient and calm. Prayer in the moment can be helpful to accomplish this.

Kindness and Goodness: This means moral goodness and uprightness — to do good or provide something beneficial for someone as an act of kindness. Because God has shown us mercy and kindness, we are called to show the same to others. Often the opportunities to show kindness are presented in unexpected ways. Whenever I see someone who appears to be in need, I listen closely for the voice of the Holy Spirit for direction. A friend shared with me an experience. She saw a gentleman outside of a convenience store who seemed to be homeless. She felt prompted to ask him if he needed anything. Surprisingly, he didn't ask for money or food. He asked for soap so he could wash his feet. My friend felt humbled to be able to bless him with a bar of soap and water. She got him a slice of pizza too. *"Never let loyalty and kindness leave you! Tie them around your neck as a reminder. Write them deep within your heart"* (Proverbs 3:3).

Faithfulness: This is a state of being someone in whom complete confidence can be placed: Trustworthiness. If you are asked to keep a secret, are you able to be trusted? When you promise to do something, do you follow through? Can your employer trust you to handle the company's money properly? In the same way that God is faithful to us, we must be faithful to others. Your reputation as a trustworthy person, a faithful friend, is essential to making meaningful connections with others.

Gentleness: Mildness in character. Jesus speaking about himself says, *"Take my yoke upon you. Let me teach you, because I am humble and gentle at heart, and you will find rest for your souls"* (Matthew 11:29). Gentleness is not the same as weakness. God does not want us to be walked on or abused. Instead we are to express ourselves gently with a quiet strength that comes from the confidence we get from our close relationship with God. *"But the wisdom from above* *is first of all pure. It is also peace-loving, gentle at all times, and willing to yield to others. It is full of mercy and the fruit of good deeds"* (James 3:17).

Self-control: This word means to exercise complete control over one's desires and actions. God calls us to holy living in 1 Peter 1:13. *"So prepare your minds for action and exercise self-control."* It is important that we do not allow ourselves to be in a situation in which we are unable to exercise self-control.

The world tells us that it is perfectly fine to drink alcohol in excess or to use recreational drugs occasionally. But the Word of God tells us we have a higher standard. In 1 Corinthians 6:12 Paul speaks to the believers in Corinth. *"You say, 'I am allowed to do anything' — but not everything is good for you. And even though 'I am allowed to do anything,' I must not become a slave to anything."* Intoxication and the abuse of mind-altering drugs have no place in the life of a Christian.

All of these characteristics require guidance and this is why God, the Holy Spirit, teaches Christians and guides them in developing the fruit. The normal response of humans in a natural state is far from the character God asks of us. Even when praying, Christians need interpretation from God, the Holy Spirit. Romans 8:26 (NIV) says, *"The Spirit helps us in our weakness. We do not know what we ought to pray for, but the Spirit himself intercedes for us through wordless groans."* The words to "I'm All In," an original on our *Christian Soul CD*, speaks to this need we have for the Holy

Spirit to intervene in our lives:

> *All that I have, all that I am*
> *All that has come, came by Your hand*
> *All that You are is more than I need*
> *All that You want, I give to Thee*

Wouldn't it be wonderful to be in a world that practiced love, joy, peace, patience, kindness, goodness, faithfulness, gentleness, and self-control? If you're a believer in Christ I want to encourage you to make sure to develop the fruit. Just like a piece of your favorite fruit, it will taste so very good to you and to others as well. Most of all it will cause God to delight in you.

FORGIVENESS

Forgiveness is the universal character of the Body of Christ. It unites us and is the very foundation of our existence. Jesus makes a profound statement after he gives the disciples the famous guide of how to pray to the Father. Matthew 6:14-15 says, *"If you forgive those who sin against you, your heavenly Father will forgive you. But if you refuse to forgive others, your Father will not forgive your sins."* If individuals do not forgive the sins of others, they cannot be saved! Forgiveness is a BIG DEAL to God.

Christians are told what to do but how is this done? Even the apostle Peter, in the Gospel of Matthew, asks Jesus how often we are to forgive. Matthew 18:21-22 says, *"Then*

Peter came to him and asked, 'Lord, how often should I forgive someone who sins against me? Seven times?' 'No, not seven times,' Jesus replied, 'but seventy times seven!'" Christians are to forgive other Christians as often as the sin is remembered. This does not mean that Christians are to let others (even other Christians) run over them and hurt them. Christians are not to be "pushovers" that allow others to abuse or belittle them. Matthew 5:38-40 says, *"You have heard the law that says the punishment must match the injury: 'An eye for an eye, and a tooth for a tooth.' But I say, do not resist an evil person! If someone slaps you on the right cheek, offer the other cheek also. If you are sued in court and your shirt is taken from you, give your coat, too."* The law for us to "offer the other cheek" and to "give your shirt" is not permission for Christians to show violence toward each other or take advantage of each other. It is a mandate for Christians to learn how to live peacefully in spite of our differences.

When Jesus said "Do not resist an evil person!" He is talking about people within your community that are close to you. They are family members or people within your church community. They are not non-believers. We are to connect and win each other over for the good. "Offer the other cheek" means forgive them when they hurt you. They will do it again, I guarantee it. Sin may not happen in the same fashion but this is the nature of humanity. We sin against each other and are in need of constant forgiveness. We forgive and then we forgive again.

Giving your shirt is not being taken advantage of. Rather

it is showing love and connection to the person regardless of the sin that they have done. It is the act of truly forgiving a person for their sin. Forgiveness can create a bond, a connection with others, that is stronger than any other.

Chapter 5

The Walk

"The Lord directs the steps of the godly. He delights in every detail of their lives. Though they stumble, they will never fall, for the Lord holds them by the hand."

Psalm 37:23-24

So, *The Lord directs the steps of the godly?* You may be thinking, "I don't think I'm 'godly'" or "I don't have a walk with God." You may not even know God. Even if you don't acknowledge God, that doesn't mean that he does not exist. But if God does exist, if he created everything and holds it all together, wouldn't you want to have a relationship with him?

I want to suggest to you that regardless of whether you

want to or not, you have a walk with the God of the universe. He has been with you from the beginning of your life until now. He is crazy about you and He wants you to know Him. He has your best interests in mind. He delights in every detail of your life. If the creator of the universe has some good plans for you, perhaps better than your plans, wouldn't you want to walk with Him?

Why all this talk about a future with God? As a Christian, you have a future with God both here on earth and eternally in heaven. We will exist in His kingdom forever and ever with others who have the same hope. What does that look like? After the death and resurrection of Jesus, He promised to come back to earth to take all who believed with Him to paradise. The Apostle Paul talks about this in his letter to the Colossians. He says, *"Since you have been raised to new life with Christ, <u>set your sights on the realities of heaven</u>, where Christ sits in the place of honor at God's right hand"* (Colossians 3:1). Christians are raised with Jesus Christ to a new life on earth. Our hope is spending eternity under the rule of Jesus as perfected bodies and souls.

I recall times that I was discontent because I wanted to do what I wanted to do. I would seek things to make me happy. I traveled, walking from one experience to another but never really feeling content. I always had the sense that I was somehow missing the mark or missing something special.

It was not until I started to walk with God and let him delight in me and I in Him, that I began to enjoy my life.

When I met my wife, Robin, I knew I needed to make a change. She wasn't going to settle for a man that was halfway committed to his faith. She motivated me to be better, to walk closer with God and I'm thankful. We've been married for 23 years and I can say that, because God has always been part of our walk together, I am a better person than I was. I began to be happy with myself. Now I have a family and I have the privilege of helping people. This is my walk with God and I've enjoyed every step. I realize that I matter to God and you do too. You can trust God with your future here on earth and eternally in heaven.

It has been hard. There are times when I stumble, and you will too. But, the joy that I experience now is so much better than what I had. God promises that He will hold me and you by the hand and He won't let us fall. This is what it means to walk with God.

Think of a small child reaching out for the parent's hand. There is a sense of security that a child has in holding on to the one who leads them. In the same way you can reach out, hold your heavenly Father's hand and trust Him to keep you from falling. Let the Lord direct you. Let him delight in you and you in him.

Take some time today. Don't wait. Get in a quiet place, away from the distractions of the world, and talk with God. You don't need to use fancy words, just talk to him about your cares. Ask Him to come into your life and direct your steps. He wants to walk with you. Tell Him you want to hold His hand and let Him lead. Over the next days and weeks you are going to be blown away by how much He cares about you and where He takes you.

Remember, the walk with God is a walk in humility. The little child must allow the parent to lead. When the child begins to struggle and make his or her own way, the walk becomes frustrating for both of them. Let God lead. This is the only way we are able to walk with God.

Chapter 6

THE DANCE

"This left Jacob all alone in the camp, and a man came and wrestled with him until the dawn began to break."

Genesis 32:24

GOD EXPECTS THOSE who believe in Him to struggle, to wrestle with Him. Can we complain to God about events that happen? Can we be real with God, our creator? The Bible says that we can. Dennis Prager, in his Rational Bible Commentary on Genesis pontificates: "Because we have the capacity to think, reason and challenge, it is impossible to go through life without questioning God about unjust suffering we see" (page 387). We may get frustrated and angry with God. We struggle with God when we don't understand why a situation is not resolved the way we thought it should be.

Existing with God is not easy, but a consistent, solid relationship with God brings purpose and meaning to life. Bringing purpose and meaning to life is one of humanity's greatest endeavors.

My Dance

I had many career changes in my life: jazz musician, classroom teacher, worship leader, and marriage and family therapist. Now I am a senior pastor. I spent a good portion of my life working to obtain a license to be a marriage and family therapist in the state of California. This desire came to me after years of teaching public school music and full time ministry in what most would call mega-churches in Southern Los Angeles. By that time I knew that I was called to help people. But my struggle with God was that I wanted to be a "jazz cat." At age fourteen, I was introduced to jazz music by my uncle and was on my way to play trumpet with the USC jazz orchestra in Germany. I listened to and imitated the album my uncle gave to me, memorizing all of the piano solos on the album, Errol Garner, *Concert by the Sea*. Though I was a trumpet player on the tour, the music on that album was the catalyst to my love for jazz music and all music.

Back to being a jazz cat. To me, a jazz cat is a musician that is recognized around the world for his or her expertise in communicating the genre of jazz to the world. My desire was to be the world's next Miles Davis or Duke Ellington. Having studied these people I understood that this lifestyle would not be pleasing to God because of my desire to fulfill my wants instead of what God wanted for me. I wanted to live the fast life of gigs, girls and good times. All of that comes with a touring jazz musician. I quickly learned that God had a better plan for me and my talents as I struggled to find a balance between a life of fast times versus a life of surrender. I stayed up night after night in my early 20s trying to figure out a way to have both a jazz career and be a good and faithful husband. I cried. I prayed. I shouted. I cursed. I wrestled. I even went to New York City to see if I could live that life. After having a great time touring NYC, I came to the end of myself and surrendered to God. It was a good time and I remained faithful to Robin and to God, but I was not satisfied by the life of a jazz cat. I wanted what God wanted for me. I came home and made a commitment to my future bride to love and cherish her. It would be hard for me to do that and be away from her, traveling and touring all over the world. I wrestled with God about it and I won. He blessed me and now I get to be married. I still play jazz music. I get to be a jazz cat, but in a different way. I am surrendered to Jesus in worship. I delighted in God and He blessed me by giving me the desires of my heart (Psalm 37:4).

Do the Dance

Turning back to our key verse from Genesis, in the morning when the struggle between God and Jacob came to an end, God said to Jacob *"Your name will no longer be Jacob...From now on you will be called Israel, because you have fought with God and with men and have won"* (Genesis 32:28). The name Israel means "struggle with God." God not only gave people permission to struggle with Him; He was actually asking us to struggle. I call that struggle "The Dance." This dance with God makes our faith authentic. And it is that authenticity which keeps us from turning into religious robots. Struggle means our relationship with God is real: Is there any person we love with whom we have never struggled? Why would it be different with God? Bestselling author, Jon Acuff said, "Wrestling with God is a sign of intimacy. You can't wrestle with someone you're far away from."

Great men and women complained in the Bible. Abraham, Sarah, Job, David, Jeremiah and Jonah complained to God. God did not strike them down. God heard their prayers and answered them. Dancing with God is not easy, but the dance with God brings purpose and meaning to life. I want to encourage you to dance with God. There is nothing wrong with it. Don't be afraid to question Him. We are allowed to do that. There are believers who think that wrestling or struggling — even questioning God, is disrespectful and irreverent. But God assures us it is not only respectful, it is expected. Simply note that we should not question him in a bitter, arrogant or profane manner.

We are invited to dance with God. Doing so makes our faith authentic. It keeps us from blindly following what we are told and causes us to strengthen our faith.

Chapter 7

THE ARMOR

"A final word: Be strong in the Lord and in his mighty power. Put on all of God's armor so that you will be able to stand firm against all strategies of the devil."

Ephesians 6:10-11

CHRISTIANS BELIEVE THAT real strength comes from God. The physically strongest man in the Bible was Samson.

God raised up judges to guide Israel after the period of Moses and Joshua. History shows that the judges start off strong with only a little variance from what God wants for them, but as time goes on, the judges of Israel tend to become less and less spiritual. Samson is born out of this now-carnal nation that has lost its connection with God and he, of course, displays a lack of obedience to God's law.

Samson was a Nazarite from birth, set apart for the Lord in a special way, and was never to eat or touch anything unclean, drink of the fruit of the vine or cut his hair (Judges 13:4-5 and Numbers 6:2-21). Samson eventually broke at least two of those commands. In addition, Samson married a Philistine woman against his parents' wishes and later lived with another Philistine woman named Delilah. This was not breaking a law but it shows that Samson was not concerned with spiritual things. He was a carnal man. This carnality eventually took his life.

One of the saddest statements in the Bible is when the Lord leaves Samson. Judges 16:18-20:

> *Delilah realized he (Samson) had finally told her the truth, so she sent for the Philistine rulers. "Come back one more time," she said, "for he has finally told me his secret." So the Philistine rulers returned with the money in their hands. Delilah lulled Samson to sleep with his head in her lap, and then she called in a man to shave off the seven locks of his hair. In this way she began to bring him down, and his strength left him. Then she cried out, "Samson! The Philistines have come to capture you!" When he woke up, he thought, "I will do as before and shake myself free." But he didn't realize the Lord had left him.*

Either Samson lost confidence in the Lord, Delilah persuaded him to exhaustion, or Samson began believing that he was the source of his strength, not God. Either way, in the end, Samson died after asking the Lord to help him defeat the Philistines one last time. It is a very sad story. Even the strongest man in the Bible could be brought down because he did not realize that his strength and help came from God.

In the New Testament, Christians are given a formula from Paul the Apostle on how to live for Christ and be bold. Paul tells of a spiritual scene that is happening in the Heavenly realm, not seen by those who are flesh and blood. He acknowledges that there is evil happening all around us. One reason for this evil is Satan. He is real. He seeks to destroy us. In the book of Job, Satan tells God that he has been *"Patrolling the earth, watching everything that's going on"* (Job 1:7, 2:2). He is a liar and an expert in deceit. He is sneaky and usually disguised as something good. Paul says in 2 Corinthians 11:14, *"Even Satan disguises himself as an angel of light."* If he came as a crazy wild spirit with horns and a pitchfork, everyone would reject him. Since he is veiled in deception, we must put on our spiritual battle gear in order to prevail. God loves us and therefore has given believers the protection we need to be able to stand against all of the strategies of Satan.

Ephesians 6:10-18, is one of the most powerful passages written by Paul. In this chapter he tells us the importance of putting on the armor of God.

> *"A final word: Be strong in the Lord and in his mighty power. Put on all of God's armor so that you will be able to stand firm against all strategies of the devil. For we are not fighting against flesh-and-blood enemies, but against evil rulers and authorities of the unseen world, against mighty powers in this dark world, and against evil spirits in the heavenly places.*
>
> *Therefore, put on every piece of God's armor so you will be able to resist the enemy in the time of evil. Then after the battle you will still be standing firm."*

Paul continues in this chapter by naming pieces of armor worn by fighting men of the day, and repurposes them for use in spiritual warfare. The urgency in his tone makes it a call to action for all believers, both of his day and ours.

The **belt of truth** protects us from Satan's lies. We can see through Satan's lies by holding them against the truth of the Bible. All of the truth represented in the Word of God is the first piece that we are to focus on. This is why regular reading and studying of the Bible is important as well as memorizing scripture verses.

The **breastplate of righteousness** guards our heart. Our heart is susceptible to the wickedness of this world, but our protection is the righteousness that comes from Jesus Christ. On our own, we can never be good enough to battle in this world. We need the one who conquered death and hell. We put on the righteousness of Jesus Christ. In Romans 13:13-14, Paul speaks more about what we need to fight against. *"Because we belong to the day, we must live decent lives for all to see. Don't participate in the darkness of wild parties and drunkenness, or in sexual promiscuity and immoral living, or in quarreling and jealousy. Instead, <u>clothe yourself with the presence of the Lord Jesus Christ</u>. And don't let yourself think about ways to indulge your evil desires."*

The **shoes of peace** protect us from Satan's traps that he uses to keep us from spreading the gospel. We are to always be ready to give a defense to everyone who asks us a reason for the hope that is in us. (1 Peter 3:15). Sharing the gospel of salvation ultimately brings peace between God and humans. We walk in the peace and love that Jesus walked in. Christians are to be the feet of Jesus, always seeking to bring peace to men.

The **shield of faith** guards us against one of Satan's deadliest weapons: doubt. Satan shoots doubt at us when God does not act immediately or visibly. But we know our Father can be counted on. Our shield of faith sends Satan's flaming arrows of doubt glancing harmlessly to the side. Faith is knowing that God exists and cares regardless of our current circumstances or feelings. The letter to the Hebrews in the New Testament tells us, *"Faith shows the reality of what we hope for; it is the evidence of things we cannot see"* (Hebrews 11:1). For the Christian, the reality of what we hope for is eternity with the GodHead — the Father, Son and Holy Spirit. The evidence of things we cannot see is the proof of God's existence and His care for us.

The **helmet of salvation** protects our minds and

represents our assurance of salvation and protection from all thoughts that may come to the contrary. The truth of salvation through Christ sets us free. We are free from vain searching, free from the meaningless temptations of this world, and free from the condemnation of sin. Our Christian conscience, the Holy Spirit, speaks to us and tells us what is right and what is wrong. We are sealed with God, the Holy Spirit, when we receive Jesus Christ as our Lord and Savior. The helmet, along with the belt, breastplate, shield and shoes, serve as our defense.

The **sword of the spirit** is the Word of God and is an offensive weapon with which we can strike Satan. When Jesus Christ was tempted by Satan, he countered with the truth of Scripture in Deuteronomy, setting an example for us. Satan's tactics have not changed, so the Sword of the Spirit is still our best defense. It is important to know that the "Word" here is referred to as a sword because it cuts with precision. Hebrews 4:12 lets us know that, *"The word of God is alive and powerful. It is sharper than the sharpest two-edged sword, cutting between soul and spirit, between joint and marrow. It exposes our innermost thoughts and desires."* It is of utmost importance to have the Word of God tell us the truth of who God is, who our enemy is and who we are. Without the Word of God, we have no strategy or offense. Therefore we must carry the Word in our minds through repetition and memorization. Joshua 1:8 makes it clear that we are to *"study this Book of Instruction continually. Meditate on it day and night so you will be sure to obey everything written in it.*

Only then will you prosper and succeed in all you do."

After we are given the elements of the armor, Paul tells us to *"Pray in the Spirit at all times and on every occasion" (Eph 6:18).* **Prayer in the Spirit** can also be considered an offensive weapon for the Christian. Prayer is a necessary aspect of Christian life and behavior. Though God is always with us, it is to our benefit to acknowledge His presence and practice faith by praying to Him. He is listening to us. 1 John 5:14-15 says, *"And we are confident that he hears us whenever we ask for anything that pleases him. And since we know he hears us when we make our requests, we also know that he will give us what we ask for."*

God not only hears us but Jesus prays for us. He told Simon Peter, *"Simon, Simon, Satan has asked to sift each of you like wheat. But I have pleaded in prayer for you, Simon, that your faith should not fail"* (Luke 22:31-32). Jesus is also praying for us right now to God the Father. Romans 8:34 says, *"Who then will condemn us? No one — for Christ Jesus died for us and was raised to life for us, and he is sitting in the place of honor at God's right hand, pleading for us."* Jesus pleads for us to God the Father in prayer. Following the example of Jesus, we pray for others and make a direct special connection to God the Father. This is our duty and our privilege as members of God's army.

It is exciting for us to know that we have weapons to accomplish God's will for our lives. Our weapons are from God and they are very mighty. 2 Corinthians 10:4-6 says, *"We use God's mighty weapons, not worldly weapons, to knock down the strongholds of human reasoning and to destroy false arguments. We destroy every proud obstacle that keeps people from knowing God. We capture their rebellious thoughts and teach them to obey Christ."*

Chapter 8

A NEW HOPE

For I know the plans I have for you," says the Lord. "They are plans for good and not for disaster, to give you a future and a hope.

Jeremiah 29:11

AS I WRITE this chapter, two stories come to my mind. The first story comes from the Star Wars franchise episode IV *A New Hope.* In 1977 the world was introduced to Luke Skywalker, a character with whom we will be enamored for the next 50 years and beyond. Then I think about my story of trying to find my place with mankind and God — wrestling and going from place to place searching for something. There is a *new hope* to find in all of us. Luke discovers who he is by discovering where he comes from and the demons he needs to confront. In my life I did the same. I confronted myself to actually find that I matter and that I have a future and a hope. Interestingly enough, the church that I now pastor is called New Hope Christian Center. God is amazing!

In the featured verse of this chapter Jeremiah the prophet is writing from a place of despair. He is called the weeping prophet because he is an eyewitness to the capturing of his people. His book Lamentations gives an account of his people, the Jews, going into captivity. Yet in the middle of his account comes a verse that you would not expect:

Because of the Lord's great love we are not consumed,
for his compassions never fail.
They are new every morning;
great is your faithfulness.
I say to myself, "The Lord is my portion;
therefore I will wait for him."
Lamentations 3:22-24 (NIV)

Jeremiah had his hope in the Lord and he was sure that the Lord was going to come through to eventually give him and his people a future and a hope.

God has that for you. He has a future for you. He wants you to be with Him. God desires to be with you today and for all of eternity. He wants you to turn to Him and enjoy your life with Him. It won't always be easy but I guarantee that life with God is better than life without God.

Let's explore what the future with God is like. Jesus gives details about the future to his disciples in the three Gospels: Matthew, Mark, and Luke. John also writes a more complete version in the book of Revelation. He describes the future:

> *Then the angel showed me a river with the water of life, clear as crystal, flowing from the throne of God and of the Lamb. It flowed down the center of the main street. On each side of the river grew a tree of life, bearing twelve crops of fruit, with a fresh crop each month. The leaves were used for medicine to heal the nations. No longer will there be a curse upon anything. For the throne of God and of the Lamb will be there, and his servants will worship him. And they will see his face, and his name will be written on their foreheads. And there will be no night there — no need for lamps or sun — for the Lord God will shine on them. And they will reign forever and ever (Revelation 22:1-4).*

What a wonderful, beautiful, peaceful place John describes! This is the future of mankind for those who believe in Jesus. However, it does not come easy. Here on earth there will be destruction and hardship like the world has never known. Massive death, plagues and pestilence will be the order of the day before Jesus comes back. Scripture tells us that no one knows the day or time when Jesus will return. Only God the Father knows (Matthew 24:36 and Mark 13:32).

There are many theories as to how this may happen and if believers in Jesus will escape or go through this time. That discussion is not within the scope of this book. What is true, though, is that the earth as we know it will be destroyed. God is going to eventually create a new heaven and a new earth and Jesus will reign over all. I want to be on the same side as the one who is going to reign forever and ever.

God's hope for you is to be with Him. The most famous verse in the Bible is John 3:16 *"For this is how God loved the world: He gave his one and only Son, so that everyone who believes in him will not perish but have eternal life."* The verse after this one is just as important because it explains God's hope for us. *"God sent his Son into the world not to judge the world, but to save the world through him."* God does not want us to suffer by being judged and separated from him. He desires to save us and spend eternity with us. That is God's hope, and this was God's plan from the beginning. Ephesians 1:4 says, *"Even before he made the world, God loved us and chose us in Christ to be holy and without fault in his eyes."*

God has a future and a hope for you. This future and hope is a gift, but you must choose to receive it. Do you want a future and a hope with Him? My journey with God has been full of wonder, adventure, mystery, joy and love but everyone's experience is different. I have found God to be who and what he says he is. In John 14:6 Jesus says, *"I am the way, the truth, and the life..."* Jesus has always been there for me and I have found Him to be loving, trustworthy, kind, patient and faithful. There is a passage in the Gospel of John where Jesus explained how he was going to suffer and die. He told the people that they needed to eat his body and drink his blood, the act of communion. He referred to himself as "the bread of life." The people took this literally and were offended by the idea of eating his body and drinking his blood. The people began to leave. When Jesus asked his disciples if they would leave too, Peter responded to Jesus. *"Lord, to whom would we go? You have the words that give eternal life. We believe, and we know you are the Holy One of God* (John 6:68-69).

I feel the same way Peter did. There is a future and a hope with Jesus in my life both now and for eternity. There is nowhere else to go but to Jesus. I truly believe this, so much so, that I want to encourage you to connect to that future and hope too.

ETERNAL LIFE

There are many people who fear death in this world. For believers, we do not need to fear death. We look forward to eternal life. Jesus gives a definition of eternal life. As he is praying to God the Father Jesus says, *"And this is the way to have eternal life — to know you, the only true God, and Jesus Christ, the one you sent to earth"* (John 17:3).

The Bible talks about death many times. The most popular scripture that talks about this is found in 1 Thessalonians 4:13-18. Paul writes to encourage the people who are fearing what will happen to them when they die. He says,

And now, dear brothers and sisters, we want you to know what will happen to the believers who have died so you will not grieve like people who have no hope. For since we believe that Jesus died and was raised to life again, we also believe that when Jesus returns, God will bring back with him the believers who have died. We tell you this directly from the Lord: We who are still living when the Lord returns will not meet him ahead of those who have died. For the Lord himself will come down from heaven with a commanding shout, with the voice of the archangel, and with the trumpet call of God. First, the believers who have died will rise from their graves. Then, together with them, we who are still alive and remain on the earth will be caught up in the clouds to meet the Lord in the air. Then we will be with the Lord forever. So encourage each other with these words.

There are many things that we can talk about in these verses, but I want to focus on the hope that we find here. It says the *"believers who have died will rise from their graves."* This means that those who believed in God will be raised from the earth and put back together in an amazing fashion as perfected beings. The scripture goes on to say… *"Then, together with them, we who are still alive and remain on the earth will be caught up in the clouds to meet the Lord in the air. Then we will be with the Lord forever."* Those who are still on earth during this time will also be transformed and meet the Lord Jesus in the air with those who passed away before them.

This is the hope of all believers. There are trials, pain, heartache, and trouble in the world. But *"in the twinkling of an eye"* (1 Cor. 15:52, NIV) it will all be over. Jesus will come and believers will be changed for good. This is the hope of life with God that the believer in Jesus can count on. Death, then, is *"swallowed up in victory"* (1 Cor. 15:54). Death has no more sting in the life of the believer.

Chapter 9

YOU HAVE IDOLS

Little children, keep yourselves from idols.
1 John 5:21 (ESV).

THE APOSTLE JOHN, who wrote a good portion of the New Testament, makes this statement after talking about sin and the believer. Jesus Christ died for us so that we may be able to flee the sin of this world that is caused, primarily, by the idols we keep. Therefore John writes, *"Keep yourselves from idols."* In other words STAY AWAY! We have idols... you have idols. When you look around this world you can clearly see that our world is full of modern day idols. The idols we have are not ordained by God. We make our own terrible substitutes and idolize them. Anything and anyone can be made into an idol. Let's take a look at the Old and New Testaments for examples.

Jeremiah 2:12-14 depicts people creating gods for themselves to worship. He equates idols to a cracked cistern that can no longer hold needed water. *"For my people have done two evil things: They have abandoned me — the fountain of living water. And they have dug for themselves cracked cisterns that can hold no water at all!"* People make idols out of things that have already been created by humans or God. These created things have no sustaining power. Only God has that power to sustain humanity and every created thing.

I made my pursuit of fame an idol. Being admired made me feel good but it did not hold water. As a trumpet player I wanted to play louder...faster...higher. The louder you play the better. The faster you can play a lick or a rift or even a classical piece the better you were as a trumpet player. The higher you can play was also the mark of a brilliant player. I wanted people to stand and cheer for me after I accomplished some technical feat. I wanted people and the music industry to cheer me instead of my relationship with God bringing me cheer...real joy. Happiness from that idol did not last. It was a broken cistern. It could not hold water. Before I knew it I had to go back to the well again.

The New King James Version of the letter to the Romans by Paul the Apostle says,

For since the creation of the world His invisible attributes are clearly seen, being understood by the things that are made, even His eternal power and Godhead, so that they are without

excuse, because, although they knew God, they did not glorify Him as God, nor were they thankful, but became futile in their thoughts, and their foolish hearts were darkened. Professing to be wise, they became fools, and changed the glory of the incorruptible God into an image made like corruptible man — and birds and four-footed animals and creeping things. Therefore God also gave them up to uncleanness, in the lusts of their hearts, to dishonor their bodies among themselves, who exchanged the truth of God for the lie, and worshiped and served the creature rather than the Creator, who is blessed forever. Amen (Romans 1:20-25).

The world says worship this. Worship that. Money, career, fame, success, pleasure, food, opulence, titles, even exercise can all be made idols. It is not God's plan that we worship these modern day things. In fact, when we do, we begin to tally what others possess and covet what they have. This breaks the 10th commandment. *"You must not covet your neighbor's house. You must not covet your neighbor's wife, male or female servant, ox or donkey, or anything else that belongs to your neighbor"* (Exodus 20:17). When we so covet, we start to compare and want more. We want his. We want hers. WE WANT IT! We are not content with what we have been given by God.

Proper worship and avoiding idol worship starts by being thankful for what God has given to you. We don't worship religion or religious activity (yes, religious activity can become an idol too!) We worship the Word, not the Bible, but the living Word, Jesus Christ. We live by the words that are expressed in the Bible but we do not worship them. *"Your word is a lamp to guide my feet and a light for my path"* Psalm (119:105). The Word of God guides the Christian. We need to fill our cistern –the one with no cracks in it – with God's living water described in the book of Jeremiah.

Psalm 90:1-2, a prayer of Moses says, *"Lord, through all the generations you have been our home! Before the mountains were born, before you gave birth to the earth and the world, from beginning to end, you are God."* God is our home. Christians believe and worship the one who feels like home. It does not feel weird for Christians to worship Jesus. It is a natural form of expression. It is the way things should be.

Chapter 10

Finding A Church

All the believers devoted themselves to the apostles' teaching, and to fellowship, and to sharing in meals, and to prayer...They worshiped together at the Temple each day, met in homes for the Lord's Supper, and shared their meals with great joy and generosity — all the while praising God and enjoying the goodwill of all the people.

Acts 2:42, 46-47

I HAVE ATTENDED many different types of churches in my lifetime. When Robin and I first got married we attended a local church. As we studied and prayed together we realized that we didn't agree with some of the teachings there. We set out to find a church that met four criteria: Sound teaching of the Word, Worship, Prayer and Fellowship with one another. These elements make a church well-rounded.

The Word

The Bible is the Word of God for the Christian. This means that the Bible is the manual of teaching for the church. If we have no manual of doctrine to follow, we are not able to function as a church body. The Bible serves as a guidebook to life and also a guidebook to the church. There are many books in the Old and New Testaments that give instruction to the believer individually, and the church or Body of Christ as a whole. Through the years the Church has interpreted these guidelines and created doctrine. Everything that we do (prayer, worship and fellowship) is based on the guidelines of scripture. Look for a church that encourages you to read the Bible on your own and also teaches, using the Bible as their primary source whenever they meet. If the ministers are using something other than the Bible as the primary source of teaching that would be a big red flag and you should look for a church elsewhere.

Worship

Worship is an expression to God from God's creation. Humans have a choice about their object of worship. We discussed previously that humans are created to worship God and that we are actually living sacrifices to God. Of course, we do not burn with fire literally, but when we worship God we burn for him figuratively. There are many forms of worship to God. Singing and musical expression are the most popular in this culture but any form of expression that brings attention to God, not self, is worship. I want to encourage you to find a church that worships God in a variety of ways, not just singing. There are churches that encourage dancing, raising your arms and clapping. All of these are acceptable as long as the one being worshiped is Jesus Christ.

Come, let us sing for joy to the Lord;
let us shout aloud to the Rock of our salvation.
Let us come before him with thanksgiving
and extol him with music and song.
For the Lord is the great God,
the great King above all gods.
In his hand are the depths of the earth,
and the mountain peaks belong to him.
The sea is his, for he made it,
and his hands formed the dry land.
Come, let us bow down in worship,
let us kneel before the Lord our Maker;
for he is our God and we are the people of his pasture,
the flock under his care (Psalm 95:1-7, NIV).

PRAYER

Prayer is our most basic form of communication with God. Communication is not one-way. God actually talks back to us. This may not be in an audible way but God always answers our prayer. The well-rounded church encourages prayer to God. Praying to God as a corporate body and as individuals is key in a well-rounded church. One aspect of prayer that is not mentioned often is reading the Bible aloud. This is also prayer. Many worship songs are prayers from the Bible. As you can start to see, these disciplines cross over in some ways and that's the point. They are supposed to cross over and mix with one another. That is what makes a well-rounded church.

FELLOWSHIP

Fellowship is intertwined with the Bible, worship and prayer. Each church will experience unique fellowship because of the ethnicities, culture and giftings in the people at any particular church. Earlier we talked about the differences that we have. Our souls are unique and God created each of us to be different from each other. The expression of our differences is most clearly seen when we come together as God's big, wonderfully diverse family and fellowship together. Hebrews 10: 25 says, *"And let us not neglect our meeting together, as some people do, but encourage one another, especially now that the day of his return is drawing near."* There is going to be a time, as our world gets closer to the return of Jesus, that you are going to need other Christians in your life even more. You must not neglect meeting together. You must have an opportunity to be encouraged and to be an encourager to other believers.

A well-rounded church gathers together on a regular basis. Some gather more than twice a week. I personally believe that gathering as a church needs to happen at least once every week. Physical contact is the best, but if that is not an option, virtual is better than none at all. By the way, church is not a building, it is a Body. If you believe in Christ, you are part of the Church body. So do not feel that you need to come to a physical building. You can do Church in the park. You can do Church in a coffee shop. You can do Church at the beach. Jesus says *"For where two or three gather together as my followers, I am there among them"* (Matt. 18:20). That is Church! That is good fellowship.

When you visit a church, look out for how they practice the four principles that I have laid out for you. All churches do not do these perfectly or in the same way. If you are looking for perfection, you will not find it in the church. Just as this world is not perfect, neither is the church. But there are some great churches out there. Keep your eyes, ears, mind and heart open to hear where God is leading you.

Chapter 11

SHARING YOUR SOUL

"Jesus called out to them, 'Come, follow me, and I will show you how to fish for people!'"

Matthew 4:19

IN MATTHEW 4, we see Jesus talking to Simon Peter and Andrew. They were brothers who fished for a living and they were very good at their craft. Jesus comes along and says "follow me." He wants them to use their gifts of fishing to fish for men. In the same way, God wants us to use the gifts that He has given us to "fish for men." We are to tell others about God's love for them and help them to accept Jesus as their Lord and Savior.

We have the ability to go out and invite people into the

kingdom for the Lord using the natural gifts we've been given. If you're a teacher, doctor, stay-at-home mom or a truck driver, use your gift for the Lord. In all you do, you can use your unique, God-given abilities to attract people to God. Jesus has given us this mission. It is the Great Commission to every believer. Jesus said, *"Go and make disciples of all the nations, baptizing them in the name of the Father and the Son and the Holy Spirit"* (Matthew 28:19).

No matter how long you have been a Christian, you are equipped with the right gifts to do the job. Some of the greatest characters in the Bible did not think that they were equipped. Moses, for example, a prince of Egypt, brought up in Pharaoh's home and raised by Pharaoh's daughter, said to God, *"Who am I to appear before Pharaoh? Who am I to lead the people of Israel out of Egypt?" (Exodus 3:11)* God does not get angry with Moses. As a matter of fact, God understood all that Moses had been through. He equipped Moses for the time he would be sent back to Egypt to lead the Hebrew people out to freedom. Moses protested two more times (Ex. 3:13 and 4:1) and when he complained of being a poor speaker, God brought in his eloquent brother, Aaron. Then God asked Moses, *"What is in your hand?" (Ex. 4:2)* This fascinating question is the same question that God asks you and me. What is in your hand? God says, I will be with you and what I have given to you as a gift is to help draw men to me. You hold your God-given gifts in your hand.

There is one more part that we must see though. Jesus encourages the disciples in the Gospel of John after his death and resurrection. Let's take a look at this story.

> *I'm going out to fish," Simon Peter told them, and they said, "We'll go with you." So they went out and got into the boat, but that night they caught nothing. Early in the morning, Jesus stood on the shore, but the disciples did not realize that it was Jesus. He called out to them, "Friends, haven't you any fish?" "No," they answered. He said, "Throw your net on the right side of the boat and you will find some." When they did, they were unable to haul the net in because of the large number of fish (John 21:3-6).*

How is it that these professional fishermen were not able to catch anything? From this story we can learn that all the acquired skills in the world are useless without God. We need God just like Moses did. We need God just like the fishermen did.

Attracting people to God is not some skill to be developed. It is a natural experience that happens as people discover God through their natural ability to communicate. You have a unique gifting to touch people in a way that no one else can. As you grow in your faith and develop your gifts, the people in your circle of influence will see subtle and sometimes major changes. Your speech patterns may change, your demeanor as you go through challenges may change, you may develop a positive attitude or you may even encourage others and appreciate them in ways you have never done before. Whatever the Holy Spirit gives you, use it for the glory of God to attract people to Him. Live your life as if someone is always watching. The most powerful example of a Christian life is when others observe the way you live when you don't think anyone is watching. Let them see Jesus in you.

INDEX
BIBLE VERSIONS

VERSES THAT DO not contain a bible version reference are from the NLT

ESV	English Standard Version
KJV	King James Version
NASB	New American Standard Bible
NIV	New International Version
NKJV	New King James Version
NLT	New Living Translation

CPSIA information can be obtained
at www.ICGtesting.com
Printed in the USA
LVHW050913030621
689238LV00018B/778